300
Incredible Things
for Home Improvement
on the
Internet

300INCREDIBLE.COM, LLC
600 Village Trace, Building 23
Marietta, Georgia 30067

(800) 909-6505

ISBN 1-930435-02-9

— Dedication —

To Margaret McGivney, dedicated science teacher and loving mother,
whose insatiable curiosity taught Janet the importance
of learning to do things herself.

Introduction

Whether buying that first house, decorating or renovating your present home or building the place of your dreams, you can benefit from helpful information available on the Internet. Discover distinguished decorator's secrets, learn how to construct a deck, purchase unique tile, examine paint samples, view architects' blueprints and even shop for a mortgage—all online. This book guides you, easily and swiftly, to the most incredible home improvement information on the Web.

Janet Pfeifer
Homeimprov123@aol.com

Ken Leebow
Leebow@300INCREDIBLE.COM
http://www.300INCREDIBLE.COM

About the Authors

Janet Pfeifer, author of several Internet books, is an avid do-it-yourselfer who has taught several home improvement, faux painting and tiling clinics at Home Depot. For Janet, how you live is as important as what you do. When she is not writing or working on a decorating project, she is out playing tennis, coaching soccer or supervising what has been referred to as "Camp Janet" (the cavorting crowd of children that gather and play in her back yard).

Ken Leebow has been involved with the computer business for over twenty years. The Internet has fascinated him since he began exploring it several years ago, and he has helped over a million readers utilize its resources. Ken has appeared frequently in the media, educating individuals about the Web's greatest hits. He is considered a leading expert on what is incredible about the Internet.

When not online, you can find Ken playing tennis, running, reading or spending time with his family. He is living proof that being addicted to the Net doesn't mean giving up on the other pleasures of life.

Acknowledgments

Putting a book together requires many expressions of appreciation. The following people deserve special thanks:

- Janet's family—her husband, for his encouragement and support; and the children (Philip, Peggy and Olivia) for keeping her grounded and making sure she had plenty of play time.

- Janet's neighbors, friends and Don Ploch, her college advisor, who in the 1980s foresaw the impact the Internet would have on society and persuaded his students to learn to use it.

- Ken's family (Denice, Alissa and Josh) for being especially supportive during the writing of the book.

- Paul Joffe and Janet Bolton, of *TBI Creative Services*, for their editing and graphics skills.

- Mark Krasner and Janice Caselli for sharing the vision of the book and helping make it a reality.

The Incredible Internet Book Series

300 Incredible Things to Do on the Internet • Volume I

300 More Incredible Things to Do on the Internet • Volume II

300 Incredible Things for Kids on the Internet

300 Incredible Things for Sports Fans on the Internet

300 Incredible Things for Golfers on the Internet

300 Incredible Things for Travelers on the Internet

300 Incredible Things for Health, Fitness & Diet on the Internet

300 Incredible Things for Auto Racing Fans on the Internet

300 Incredible Things for Self-Help & Wellness on the Internet

300 Incredible Things to Learn on the Internet

300 Incredible Things for Home Improvement on the Internet

America Online Web Site Directory
Where to Go for What You Need

TABLE OF CONTENTS

TABLE OF CONTENTS (continued)

CHAPTER I
STARTING TO IMPROVE

1
Home Depot

http://www.homedepot.com

Whether you are a seasoned do-it-yourselfer, weekend warrior or a frequent caller to Mister Fixit, you can benefit from Home Depot's expert "how to" advice. This site even helps you create personal project files.

2
Lowe's

http://www.lowes.com

You can find plenty of professional tips, advice and inspiration for home projects here, including a seasonal maintenance checklist and many problem-solving solutions.

3
HGTV

http://www.hgtv.com

If you enjoy learning to live the good life by watching HGTV, you'll have fun at its Web site, a virtual clearinghouse of ideas and projects for your home and garden.

4
Home Improvement Encyclopedia

http://www.bhglive.com/homeimp

This is a fantastic improvement reference for the do-it-yourselfer. Learn how to do almost anything around the house with the easy-to-use guides at this site.

5
ImproveNet

http://www.improvenet.com

Indulge your design ideas. Access thousands of products with a quick click at this home improvement powerhouse.

6
Project Calculators

http://www.homeideas.com/applets
http://www.homedepot.com/cgi-bin/prel80/calculators/index.jsp
http://www.bhglive.com/homeimp/calculators/index.html
http://www.allabouthome.com/calculators/index.html

Save yourself a few trips to the store by accurately measuring and estimating your job needs before you buy. These calculators help you figure how much stuff you'll need for painting, laying grass seed, applying fertilizer and dozens of other projects.

7
Home Solutions

http://www.todayshomeowner.com
http://www.ahahome.com
Efficiently manage your household with new home improvement tips offered everyday.

8
Bob Vila Online

http://www.bobvila.com
There are lots of ingenious ideas from a seasoned professional at this Web site. If you're stumped by a particularly difficult project, ask Bob and receive an answer.

9
Your Home

http://www.hometime.com
Point, print and set yourself to work on one of the many delightful projects offered at this site, sponsored by the award-winning PBS Television show.

10
Home Tips

http://www.hometips.com
http://www.ehow.com
Launch a new project, tackle your home improvement troubles or analyze the product buying guides at this site.

11
Fun Projects

http://www.diynet.com

Gain quick and easy access to hundreds of unique design ideas, from uptown elegance to country crafty.

12
Home Away from Home

http://www.homearts.com

Kick off your shoes and stay a while. This site is a cozy Web community for gracious home living with many articles on home improvement, gardening, decorating and design.

13
House Chat

http://www.housenet.com

Find unique solutions to your decorating dilemmas or share your home improvement success stories in one of the many chat rooms at this site.

14
Home Store

http://www.homestore.com

This site is chock full of clever tips on home buying, financing, decorating and shopping.

15
Home Improvement Advice for Women and Men

http://www.theremodelinggal.com
http://www.theremodelingguy.com
http://www.naturalhandyman.com

Experience these quick and easy improvement references. One is filled with articles on home improvement for women, the other for men.

16
Consumer Reports

http://www.consumerreports.org

Receive free advice about the quality of products and product safety features. To receive the detailed reports and buying recommendations, you must join—for only $3.95 a month.

17
Federal Consumer Publications

http://www.pueblo.gsa.gov/housing.htm

Let tax dollars help save you money and hassles. Compliments of Uncle Sam, a vast number of informational brochures for the homeowner are at your fingertips.

18
Buying Guides

http://www.consumersdigest.com
http://www.productreviewnet.com
http://www.consumerworld.org
http://consumer.checkbook.org/consumer/index/homeimprovement.htm
Become an educated consumer. Read buying advice, discover the best bargains and analyze the product reviews within these sites.

19
How Things Work

http://www.howthingswork.com
http://www.learn2.com
Avoid a repair fiasco. Find out exactly how things in your house work, before taking them apart.

CHAPTER II
INTERIOR DECORATING AND DESIGN

20
Decorating Advice

http://www.bhg.com/househome
Track new trends and join discussion groups on decorating, household management, seasonal celebrations and decorations.

21
What's Your Style?

http://www.villagehome.com/DrDecor/DrDecor.htm
http://housebeautiful.women.com
Take these quick quizzes to find your style, then view samples and suggestions that show how to put your preferences to work in your home.

22
Decorating Secrets

http://www.decoratorsecrets.com
Benefit from the knowledge of professional decorators. Sign up for a free newsletter to keep up with ever-changing decorating trends.

23
Be Your Own Decorator

http://www.decoratewaverly.com

Decorate like a pro with the help of comprehensive project guides, expert recommendations and home decorating patterns available at this site. Use the product locator to find the perfect coordinating fabric for your next project.

24
Hire an Interior Decorator

http://www.interiors.org

The American Society of Interior Designers provides this free nationwide referral service of decorators who are professionally trained, tested and accredited.

25
Martha Stewart

http://www.marthastewart.com

If you have the time, Martha Stewart has a lovely decorating project for you. As Martha says, "It's a good thing!"

26
Virtual Decorating

http://www.seemydesign.com
http://www.designaroom.com
http://www.totalhomenetwork.com
Design dream rooms without spending a penny, and experiment with paint colors and techniques without spilling a drop.

27
Traditional Decorating Ideas

http://housebeautiful.women.com
http://www.southernliving.com
Does your style tend toward the traditional? These sites help you perfect that timeless and classic look.

28
Contemporary Flair

http://www.m-pm.com
http://www.unicahome.com
http://www.retromodern.com
http://www.guild.com
http://www.gomod.com
http://www.decotodisco.com
http://www.jetsetmodern.com
If you prefer eclectic, art deco or retro, you'll enjoy the tips and products at these sites.

29
Italian Design

http://www.italydesign.com
http://www.mktweb.it/arredando
http://www.trident.nettuno.it/Mall/PVS/PVS.html
http://www.online.it/expo/indice.html
These sites offer distinctive products with Old World style and Mediterranean allure.

30
Country Charm

http://www.countryliving.com
http://www.sampler.com/decideas/decideas.html
http://www.countrycurtains.com
Country crafts, decorations and products abound at these sites.

31
People like You

http://www.thathomesite.com
Discuss and exchange decorating ideas with people just like yourself. Choose among many forums, including art, home office, cleaning, cooking, parenting and more to find a group that shares your interests and tastes.

32
Feng Shui

http://www.fengshuiguild.com
http://www.xdimension.com/fengshui
Learn the principles of this ancient Oriental approach to decorating and design that has recently become the rage of the Western World — then clear the clutter and transform your home into a tranquil sanctuary.

33
Decorating Children's Rooms

http://www.benjaminmoore.com/past-projects/chalkboard.html
http://www.landofnod.com
http://www.preciousplaces.com
http://www.laura-ashley.com
http://www.landsend.com
http://www.thecompanystore.com
http://www.kidcarpet.com

These sites can help you create a stimulating and magical environment for your little ones.

34
Buy Art

http://www.paintingsdirect.com
http://www.art.com
http://www.artuframe.com
http://www.hi100.artselect.com

Click a picture, any picture. These sites let you pick the perfect painting, print, poster or photo for your home. Learn about different styles of art, and discover tips for framing pictures yourself. You can even create your own online art gallery.

35
Commission Art Reproductions

http://www.famousartreproductions.com
http://www.oldmaster-paintings.com
http://www.tuscanyfinearts.com
http://www.isabel.com

Order museum quality reproductions of many famous paintings with the easy to use, search-by-artist selections at these sites.

36
Stencil It

http://www.dresslerstencils.com

View hundreds of stencils to get ideas for a custom finished look. The motifs range from the deserts of Africa to dense Woodland Gardens. Complete directions guide your way.

"Are you sure you want me to fix up the house?
If we let it go another year or two, it will
qualify as 'rustic charm'!"

37
Shop for Decorative Accessories

http://www.ballard-designs.com
http://www.myhome.com
http://www.restorationhardware.com
http://www.goodhome.com
http://accessorypoint.homepoint.com
http://www.crateandbarrell.com
http://www.10thavenue.com
http://www.pier1.com
http://www.spiegel.com
http://www.target.com

Looking for unique accessories for your home? Use these secure sites to locate and buy novel home accessories, uncommon hardware and basic decorating supplies.

38
When Ordinary Won't Do

http://www.ebay.com

Do you need a one-of-a-kind knick-knack to add the finishing touch to your décor? Try this online auction—you'll find it here, if anywhere. Some friends just purchased papyrus prints direct from a Middle Eastern artist for their Egyptian room.

39
Home Product Locator

http://www.homeportfolio.com
This is a clearinghouse for thousands of premium design products. View online brochures
from leading manufacturers, and save your favorites in a personal portfolio.

40
Manufacturer's Brochures

http://www.homeideas.com
Would you like to review product information at your leisure? Pick and click before you
decorate, to receive product brochures by mail.

41
Find Discontinued Fabric

http://www.web-decor.com
Locate discontinued fabric, and use the yardage chart to determine how much fabric you
need for reupholstering chairs and sofas.

42
Architectural Salvage
http://www.architecturalsalvagevt.com
http://www.architectural-salvage.com
http://www.recyclingthepast.com
http://www.arcsalve.ie
http://oldhousesalvage.com
They may not make stuff like they used to, but now you can search for that stuff all over the world. Add distinction to your home and grounds with architectural salvage.

43
Decorate on a Budget
http://www.hgtv.com/shows/DCT.shtml
http://www.suite101.com/welcome.cfm/low_budget_decorating
Create a new look for next to nothing when you discover the helpful hints and money-saving ideas at these thrifty sites.

44
Silk Plants, Trees and Dried Flowers
http://www.silkplants.net
http://www.theflowermart.com
Add color and fragrance to your home with dried flowers. They look beautiful, and you don't need to water them.

45
Flower Arranging

http://www.lhj.com/yourhome/flowers
http://www.floralhome.com
Experience grace and beauty by learning to aesthetically arrange and display flowers.

46
Practical Advice

http://www.pdra.org/dr/articles
Read professional decorating articles, and test your knowledge of color. Find out how using different colors can affect your mood.

CHAPTER III
WALLS AND WINDOWS

47
Paint School

http://www.ppgaf.com/school.htm
http://www.paintquality.com
http://www.paint.org/con_info/brochures.htm
Learn to paint like a professional at these instructive sites.

48
Faux Painting

http://www.fauxlikeapro.com
http://www.benjaminmoore.com/d/d4.html
http://wallsalive.com/protip3.html
It's amazing what you can do with a can of paint. Uncover the secrets to successful faux effects like marbleizing, sponging, ragging and glazing.

49
Paint Brands

http://www.behrpaint.com
http://www.benjaminmoore.com
http://www.ppgaf.com
http://www.gliddenpaint.com
http://www.sherwin.com
http://www.acehardware.com/paintbrand/paintbrand.asp
http://www.devoepaint.com
These Web sites offer exceptional information about paint and decorating with paint.
Search for your favorite colors online.

50
Paint Problems Q&A

http://www.pdra.org/FAQs/paint
Find answers to your painting problems here.

51
Choosing a Paint Applicator

http://www.pdra.org/FAQs/paint-applicators
http://www.generalpaint.com/tools.html
http://www.shadesofcolor.com/paintappfaq.htm
Get advice for choosing the right size and type of roller or brush for your next paint job.

52
Do-it-Yourself Residential Wallpaper Guide
http://www.wallcoverings.org/residential/index.html
Learn about changing trends, how much to buy and proper cleaning methods.

53
Wall Covering FAQ&A
http://www.pdra.org/FAQs/wallcoverings
Explore a wide range of wall coverings at this site, and study your options of hiring someone or doing it yourself.

54
Wallpaper Hanging Basics
http://www.paperhanging.com/class
Before you open the first roll, learn all about how to successfully hang wallpaper.

55
Removing Old Wallpaper
http://www.learn2.com/05/0527/0527.php3
http://www.todayshomeowner.com/repair/19971074.home.html
Use these helpful, step-by-step instructions for removing all types of stubborn wallpaper from your home.

56
Decorate with Borders
http://www.wallpaperguide.com/index3.htm
For a new look, try dressing up a room with wallpaper borders.

57
Wallpaper Murals
http://www.wallsofthewild.com
http://lelandswallpaper.com/murals.htm
When wallpaper isn't enough, try one of these murals for a look that's really unique.

58
Shop for Wallpaper Online
http://www.abwf.com
http://www.lelandswallpaper.com
http://www.wallpaperplus.com
http://www.americandrapery.com
There are thousands of wallpaper styles, blinds, stencils and murals, all available for viewing and purchasing online.

59
Blinds and Window Coverings

http://www.levolor.com
http://www.hunterdouglas.com
http://www.nobrainerblinds.com
http://www.shuttersinc.com
http://www.blindsgalore.com
http://www.blindswholesale.com
http://www.1blinds.com

Search these sites, and explore the many types and colors of blinds, shutters and shades.

60
Create Curtains Online

http://www.curtainrods.com
http://housebeautiful.women.com/hb/decorate/windows/00intr11.htm

Choose from hundreds of decorative rods, hardware and fabrics, then design custom window treatments in a few clicks.

61
Drapery Ideas

http://www.draperypro.com/DreamWindowsPage1.htm

View a gallery of award-winning draperies created by professionals around the country.

62
Window and Door Basics

http://www.doorandwindow.com/Howto.html
http://www.doors-windows.com
Learn about different types of windows and doors, how to repair them and how to measure for and install replacements.

63
Best Windows for Your Climate

http://www.efficientwindows.org
Certain types of windows work better in particular climates. Select your state, and read a fact sheet that will help you choose the best windows for your region.

64
Window and Door Manufacturers

http://www.andersencorp.com
http://www.marvin.com
http://www.pella.com
http://www.caradco.com
http://www.pozzi.com
http://www.velux.com
http://www.peachtreedoor.com
http://www.iwpdoor.com
http://www.lifetimedoors.com
http://www.steelcraft.com
http://www.premdor.com
http://www.forever.com
You won't believe the options. Search for the windows and doors of your dreams.

65
Custom Windows and Doors

http://www.hhirschmannltd.com
When ordinary won't do, check out these custom-made windows and doors.

66
Surplus Doors and Windows
http://www.buildersexpress.com
Search for surplus doors and windows, and maybe you'll swing a deal.

67
How to Hang or Repair a Door
http://www.hometime.com/projects/howto/windoor/pc2wd03.htm
http://www.oldhouseweb.net/stories/How-To/Doors
It's tricky to hang a door just right, so learn how to do it from professionals. You can also discover how to fix and patch most types of doors.

68
Garage Doors
http://www.amarr.com
http://www.clopaydoor.com
http://www.raynor.com
http://www.gadco.com
http://www.wayne-dalton.com
http://www.doormart.com
http://www.geniecompany.com
At these sites, you can preview your garage door choices.

CHAPTER IV
KITCHENS AND BATHS

69
National Kitchen and Bath Association

http://www.nkba.org/consumer.html

Consider the details when designing or remodeling your kitchen or bath. Read a collection of articles about lifestyle, safety, layout and traffic flow.

70
Kitchen and Bath Ideas

http://www.kitchen-bath.com

This virtual clearinghouse for kitchen and bath ideas has something for everyone. Study new product reviews, comparison discussions, buyer's guides and find answers to some frequently asked questions.

71
Kitchen Planning

http://www.bhg.com/kpg

Plan your kitchen like a pro, after you review the most popular kitchen layouts. Find out how to choose quality cabinets and consider up-to-date kitchen trends in this idea gallery.

"Who says floppy disks are obsolete?
They make great bathroom tiles!"

72
Design a Custom Kitchen Online
http://www.improvenet.com/plan/visualize/kitchens/index.html
http://www.kitchen-design.com
Plan a new kitchen online — complete with appliances — before you start shopping around.

73
Remodeling Kitchens and Baths
http://www.todayshomeowner.com/kitchen/index.html
Read informative articles that contain objective advice at this site.

74
Kitchen Cabinet Manufacturers Association
http://www.kcma.org
This site can help you select the right cabinets, based upon your tastes and needs.

75
Cabinet Manufacturers

http://www.americanwoodmark.com
http://www.kraftmaid.com
http://www.millspride.com
http://www.canackitchens.com
http://www.kitchencraft.com
http://www.merillat.com
http://www.aristokraft.com
http://www.signaturecab.com
You can tour dozens of kitchen galleries online, thanks to these cabinet manufacturers.

76
Association of Home Appliance Manufacturers

http://www.aham.org
This consumer guide gives practical advice to help you select, operate, maintain and repair all of your household appliances.

77
Appliance Manufacturers

http://www.amana.com
http://www.ge.com
http://www.dacorappl.com
http://www.kitchenaid.com
http://www.maytag.com
http://www.sears.com/kenmore/new.htm
http://www.thermador.com
http://www.viking-range.com
http://www.whirlpool.com
Search for appliances and review product specifications at these manufacturers' Web sites.

78
Countertop Choices

http://southernliving.com/homes/countertop.asp
Understand different countertop surface materials. Explore the pros and cons of each counter type, and compare prices at this site.

79
Countertop Manufacturers

http://www.wilsonart.com
http://www.dupont.com/corian
http://www.formica.com
http://www.theswancorp.com/swanstone.html
http://www.awp.net
http://www.findstone.com
http://www.designergranite.com
http://www.mrdgranite.com
http://www.arkardystudios.bigstep.com
Entertain all of your countertop options. View laminate, solid surface, wood, stone and concrete counters at these manufacturers' and suppliers' sites.

80
Faucets, Sinks, Whirlpools and Tubs

http://www.deltafaucet.com
http://www.kohlerco.com/kitchenbathindex.html
http://www.pricepfister.com
http://www.moen.com
http://www.masco.com
http://www.us.amstd.com
http://www.groheamerica.com
http://www.peerless-faucet.com
http://www.jacuzzi.com
Try out the new faucets and bathtubs at these sites.

81
Shop for Kitchen and Bath Accessories

http://www.bedbathandbeyond.com
http://www.cooking.com
http://www.jcpenny.com
http://www.kitchenandhome.com
http://www.sears.com
http://www.williams-sonoma.com
http://www.target.com
http://www.walmart.com

Perk up your kitchen or bath with something new from these secure online retailers.

82
Remodel Your Bath

http://www.bathwise.com
http://www.bathweb.com

These sites provide access to over 20,000 products for the bath and kitchen, with links to manufacturers, consumer services, plumbing, decorative hardware and accessories.

83
Spa FAQ
http://www.siouxlan.com/spas/faq.html
Thinking of a spa? Find out how much it will cost and decide whether you want one that's in the ground, portable or indoor.

84
Spa Showroom
http://www.hotspringspa.com
http://www.sundancespas.com
Visit these virtual showrooms to find a spa that fits your desires and budget.

85
Plumbing School
http://www.bhglive.com/homeimp/plumbing.html
Before you call the plumber, you might consider fixing it yourself. At this site, you can get basic training in plumbing repair and maintenance.

86
Cyber Plumbers

http://www.theplumber.com
http://www.plbg.com
Here's plenty of advice about plumbing in kitchens, baths and all things that move water through your home.

87
Plumbing Supplies

http://www.plumbshop.com
http://www.plumbingworld.com
http://www.plumbingsupply.com
http://www.plumbingwarehouse.com
You'll find one-stop shopping for your plumbing needs at these sites. Browse through the many available products and gather ideas for redesigning your kitchen or bath.

88
Solve Common Water Problems

http://www.wqa.org
http://www.siouxlan.com/water/faq.html
http://edis.ifas.ufl.edu/AE009
Learn about major water problems, and what you can do about them. Learn how to test your water and uncover possible solutions to hard water, stinky water and disease.

89
Water Saving Tips

http://www.americanwater.com/49ways.htm
Save thousands of gallons of water a year when you follow the advice of this leading manufacturer, who can show you some quick, do-it-yourself plumbing repairs and upgrades.

CHAPTER V
FLOORING AND TILE

90
<u>All About Tile</u>

http://www.infotile.com
http://www.tilebiz.com
From the ordinary to the unusual, find answers to all of your questions about tile. There are also links to manufacturers' online catalogs around the world.

91
<u>Tile Pattern Guide</u>
http://www.daltile.com/daltile/tile_pattern_guide/tile_layout_guide.html
Add a refined look to your room by laying tile in unique and interesting patterns.

92
Find Tile

http://www.am-marazzi.com
http://www.aotile.com
http://www.floridatile.com
http://www.daltile.com
http://www.alphatile.com
http://www.laufen.com
Search some popular manufacturers' sites to find ideas and the right tile for your home.

93
Unique Tiles

http://www.annsackstile.com
http://www.creativetileworks.com
http://www.tiles.org/pages/studios.htm
http://www.batiktile.com
http://www.artistictile.net
Want distinctive tile—hand painted or bas-relief? View beautiful, one-of-a-kind tiles online.

94
Fine Stone Products

http://www.findstone.com

If you appreciate the beauty of natural stone, visit this informative site to view hundreds of stone products, from tiles to statues. Learn about defects to avoid, and decide whether this rich, natural product is for you.

95
Installing Tile

http://www.infotile.com/features/installing/contents.html

Choose the right tile and get detailed instructions on how to prepare and install.

96
All About Flooring

http://www.floorbiz.com

Explore over 500 flooring options, and discover the kind that is best for your home.

97
Laminate Flooring

http://www.floorbiz.com/learn/laminate-middle.htm

http://www.floorsearch.com/laminate/laminate.html

Learn why laminate flooring is growing in popularity and how it is engineered to last. Read articles comparing the brands, and learn how to install and care for a laminate floor.

98
Flooring Manufacturers
http://www.floorfacts.com
You'll find direct links to flooring manufacturers' online catalogs and product information listings. Search by flooring type, including bamboo, laminate, vinyl, wood and carpet.

99
Installing Vinyl Flooring
http://www.buildbiz.com/directory/Learn-Products.asp?CategoryID=12
Modern vinyl tiles are not like those that were in your mother's kitchen. Discover your options and learn how to install and repair vinyl floors.

100
National Wood Flooring Association
http://www.woodfloors.org
Explore the many choices available in hardwood flooring, from finish, grain, grade and width, to inlaid designs with different species of wood. Learn their unique characteristics and how to care for hardwood floors.

101
Refinishing Hardwood Floors
http://www.todayshomeowner.com/repair/19990915_feature2.html
Learn how to refinish and restore hardwood flooring.

"How can we redecorate the bathroom when we can't even agree on which way the toilet paper should unroll?"

102
Carpet and Rug Institute
http://www.carpet-rug.com
Find answers to your questions about carpet, including installation tips, carpet care and cleaning. Learn how to gauge carpet quality by understanding a carpet's durability rating.

103
Carpet FAQ&A
http://www.pdra.org/FAQs/floorcoverings
Find out how the cut, loop, twist and fiber content of carpet affects its resistance to wear.

104
Carpet Cleaning Tips
http://www.a2zresources.com
Learn how to keep your carpet looking new for years to come.

105
Avoid Carpet Scams
http://www.teleport.com/~jag/install.html
Choose the best carpet pad, and avoid being scammed at the carpet store.

106
Guides to Collecting Fine Rugs
http://www.sothebys.com/connoisseur/guides/rugs_tex/rugs
http://tehran.stanford.edu/Images/Persian_Carpet/carpet.html
You won't find a flying carpet, but with Sotheby's expert advice about rugs, you may land a timeless treasure for your home. Don't forget to check out the online auctions.

107
Karastan
http://www.karastan.com
View affordable, wool luxury Persian and Oriental carpet and rug collections. If you like what you see, this site will locate a dealer in your area.

CHAPTER VI
LIGHTING AND ELECTRIC

108
Lighting
http://www.homelighting.com
Read about current lighting trends while you search this comprehensive collection of lighting links. Click on items of interest, and you'll be provided with manufacturers' names and addresses. You won't find a genie, but you might find a magical lamp for your home.

109
A Guide to Lighting
http://www.lrc.rpi.edu/Ltgtrans/HomeLtg/index.htm
http://www.northwestlighting.com/residential/index.html
Consider these room-by-room tips for planning better lighting in your home.

110
Lamp Shopping

http://www.lampdepot.com
http://www.lamphouse.com
http://www.lamp-fashions.com
http://www.lampsontheweb.com
http://www.magicmushroomlamps.com
From the timeless tiffany to the "groovy" lava, all sorts of lamps can be found and purchased at these sites.

111
Let There Be Light

http://www.bulbs.com
http://www.askdrbulb.com
Does an inexpensive light bulb really save you money? Find out here, where you can purchase hard-to-find light bulbs, and get professional answers to your lighting questions.

112
Ceiling Fans

http://www.faninfo.com
http://www.hunterfan.com
http://www.casablancafanco.com
http://www.emersonfans.com
Search these online catalogs for fans, air purifiers, thermostats or humidifiers, and locate a dealer near you.

113
Air Conditioning and Heating

http://www.hvacmall.com
http://www.doityourself.com/hvac
http://www.improvenet.com/page2/heatingventilation.html
http://www.improvenet.com/page2/air_conditioning.html
These are practical guides to heating, ventilation and air conditioning. You can find manufacturers' and consumer information, view products and much more.

114
Home Improvement Wiring Index

http://www.bhglive.com/homeimp/wiring.html
Don't get zapped! The next time you wire, or rewire, check with this wiring guide first.

115
Electrical Safety List
http://www.pueblo.gsa.gov/press/electric.htm
Learn how to conduct a complete home electrical safety check.

116
Energy Efficiency
http://www.doityourself.com/electric
Is your home energy efficient? Find out.

117
Energy Efficient Appliances
http://www.energystar.gov
Search for products that are guaranteed to use less energy, from special light bulbs to insulation. All of these products are Energy Star approved.

118
Appliance Buying Guides

http://www.appliance.com
http://www.applianceadvisor.com/brandadvisor.htm
http://www.aham.org/indexconsumer.htm
http://www.brandwise.com

Get the inside scoop before shopping for your next appliance. Review new products and buying guides to find what's best for your family.

119
No-nonsense Electrical Tips

http://www.allabouthome.com/directories/dir_electrical.html
http://members.tripod.com/~masterslic/electritian.html

Know what to check the next time your power goes out. Read these home electrical tips.

120
Home Theater

http://htbg.supersites.net
http://www.sdinfo.com
http://www.guidetohometheater.com
http://www.digitaltheater.com

Learn home theater design basics, and optimize your acoustics. Examine the latest home theater products at these Web sites.

121
<u>Wired Home</u>
http://my.ohio.voyager.net/~dhoehnen/ha/list.html
If it pertains to home automation, it's probably linked to this sweeping site.

122
<u>Shopping for Home Automation</u>
http://www.smarthome.com
http://www.hometoys.com
http://www.homecontrols.com
http://www.electronichouse.com/hotprod.shtml
Shop for home automation tools and toys at these sites.

CHAPTER VII
LANDSCAPING AND RECREATION

123
Gardening

http://www.garden.com
Get the dirt on gardening and landscaping at this fun and resourceful site.

124
Virtual Gardener

http://www.virtualgarden.com
Here's a user-friendly community of gardening advice, regional tips, to-do-lists and links to address your gardening needs.

125
Garden Club

http://www.bhglive.com/gardening
You'll feel like you've joined a garden club at this site, with friendly advice on choosing the best plants for your yard, a searchable plant index and professional articles for better landscaping.

126
Garden Exchange
http://www.gardenweb.com
This search engine offers forums for exchanging ideas with other gardening enthusiasts.

127
Check the Weather
http://www.weather.com/gardening
Don't be left out in the cold. Find out your local forecast, plan your outdoor time and discover new gardening tips at the same time.

128
Farmers' Almanac
http://www.farmersalmanac.com/gardening/gardening.html
If you like to plant in harmony with lunar phases, use the monthly gardening calendar at this site to stay in tune with the moon.

129
Landscape Design
http://clearwaterlandscapes.com/index.htm
http://aggie-horticulture.tamu.edu/extension/homelandscape/home.html
With free landscape design and maintenance advice from experienced landscapers, these sites help you choose the right plants with your long-term goals in mind.

130
Lawn Mowers and Trimmers
http://www.whatsthebest-lawnmower.com
Lawn mowers and trimmers are reviewed in detail here. Find the best one for you.

131
What's Your Zone?
http://www.vg.com/gemag/s=4536
http://www.ars-grin.gov/ars/Beltsville/na/hardzone/ushzmap.html
http://www.plantadviser.com
Determine your geographical zone and pick the plants that will flourish in your climate.

132
Garden Planning
http://www.bhg.com/bhggarden/gardenplans/preview.html
Use this comprehensive guide to plan beautiful and varied landscapes.

133
Before You Plant
http://www.gardenguides.com
This is an indispensable resource for growing impressive flowers, vegetables and herbs.

134
Plant Guide
http://www.lowes.com/lowes/findex.asp
This plant guide contains useful information for growing healthy plants, shrubs and trees.

135
Call before You Dig
http://www.contractors.com/h_resources/callb4udig.html
Don't spring a leak! Call your utilities so they can mark their lines before you start to dig. The appropriate numbers are listed by state at this site.

136
Ask Earl, the Yard Care Answer Guy
http://www.yardcare.com
Find answers to your yard care dilemmas. Ask a question or study the pre-set topics.

137
Grow Beautiful Bulbs
http://www.bulb.com
You'll never be without blooms again. Use this planting guide to determine when, where and what kind of bulbs to plant next.

138
Growing Herbs
http://www.wholeherb.com
Spice up your life, grow herbs. Learn how to plant and care for your favorites — parsley, sage, rosemary and thyme.

139
Attract Butterflies to Your Garden
http://www.si.edu/resource/tours/gardens/butterfly
http://www.mnsinc.com/cornucopia/gp9706.htm
Find out which plants attract certain butterflies.

140
Garden Party
http://www.mnsinc.com/cornucopia/gardpart.htm
Each month, you'll learn something new, like how to make the most of your mulch, which bulbs to plant in the spring or how to grow plants from seed.

141
Annuals
http://discoveringannuals.com/az.html
Determine the right amount of sun, the proper pH level and more to foster healthier annuals.

142
Perfect Perennials

http://www.pbs.org/perennialgardener
Plant and maintain beautiful flowers that will thrive for years to come.

143
Weed Control and Soil Management

http://www.ag.ohio-state.edu/~ohioline/lines/hygs.html
Here's advice on soil testing, pesticides and fertilizers for maintaining an emerald lawn.

144
Vegetable Gardens

http://www.kitchengardener.com
http://www.naturalland.com/gv/ffg/ffg.htm
http://gardenguides.com/Vegetables/vegetabl.htm
Grow your own veggies. You'll learn how at these sites

145
Organic Gardening

http://www.organicgardening.com
Everything you need to know about maintaining an organic garden is here. Learn about the genetic engineering of food and its possible harmful effects.

146
Composting
http://www.vegweb.com/composting
Make the most of your garbage by learning how to compost.

147
Plant Encyclopedia
http://homearts.com/affil/gardb/main/plantf1.frm
Will talking to your plants will help them grow? Find out.

148
Roses
http://www.rose.org
http://www.timelessroses.com
http://www.everyrose.com
You can grow winning roses. Learn how at these Web sites that provide experienced advice on planting, caring for and designing a bed of roses.

149
Orchids
http://www.orchidweb.org
This exotic flower's secrets are revealed here.

150
Clematis
http://www.homeofclematis.com
A Clematis is a climbing perennial with many large, colored blooms. It's perfect for your mail box, lamp post or trellis. Learn how to choose and care for your Clematis here.

151
Tropical Hibiscus
http://www.trop-hibiscus.com
Cultivate this amazing plant that comes in a colorful rainbow of blooms.

152
Propagation
http://www.ghg.net/beyer/propag.htm
Learn how to grow plants from leaf, stem and root cuttings. The experts have special tricks, and you can find many of them here.

153
Helpful Bugs
http://www.natural-insect-control.com
http://www.bugstore.com
Control insect predators and plant diseases with anti-bug bugs. These sites show you how to make neighborly insects your garden's best friend.

154
Seed School

http://www.seedsonline.com
Attend this online Seed School before you plant. You'll be successful the next time you try to grow from a packet.

155
Garden Tools

http://www.gardenreview.com/reviews
Read reviews to determine which garden tool is right for your project. Submit your own reviews of your favorite — or not-so-favorite — garden tools.

156
National Gardening Association

http://www.garden.org
Find out about garden events in your local area, and check out the buying guide for links to great gardening products online.

157
Water It

http://www.irrigation.org
http://www.rainbird.com
http://www.netyard.com/jsa/spklr.htm
http://www.jessstryker.com
Greener pastures lay ahead. Everything you need to know about irrigating your garden and lawn can be found at these sites.

158
Pondering a Pond?

http://www.pondandgarden.com
http://www.vnwg.com
http://www.gardenweb.com/forums/ponds
http://members.home.net/crush11
http://www.watergarden.com
Learn how to create and maintain your own backyard oasis. No fishing poles allowed!

159
Something's Fishy

http://www.kencofish.com
http://www.vcnet.com/koi_net
Now that you're inspired to build a pond, find some exotic fish to swim in it.

160
Carnivorous Plants

http://www.sarracenia.com
Goodbye, fly! Observe these mysterious plants, and find out where you can buy them.

161
Tree Care

http://www.sufa.com
http://www.teleport.com/~pnwisa/tree-care.html
http://www2.champaign.isa-arbor.com/consumer/consumer.html
What you need to grow hearty trees can be found at these timber-touting sites — planting
guides, pruning directions, a tree care calendar, how to select healthy trees and more.

162
Design Your Hardscapes

http://www.clearwaterlandscapes.com/hardscapes.htm
Add some architectural design to your landscape.

163
Fences and Gates

http://www3.hometime.com/projects/howto/lawngrdn/pc2lgfen.htm
http://www.petsafe.net
Everything you need to know about planning, installing, and maintaining visible and invisible fences around your property.

164
Creating A Brick Walkway or Patio

http://muextension.missouri.edu/xplor/agguides/hort/g06930.htm
Lay a walkway or border to enhance your landscaping. It's simple with this online guide.

165
Play Structures

http://www.cedarworks.com
http://www.rainbowplay.com
http://www.creativeplaythings.com
http://www.swing-n-slide.com
With do-it-yourself play sets, custom designs, shipping and installation instructions, your play structure desires can be met at these sites.

166
Gardening with Children
http://www.geocities.com/EnchantedForest/Glade/3313
http://aggie-horticulture.tamu.edu/kindergarden/index.html
Share gardening with your little ones, and you'll teach them to care for their world. They will be growing their own vegetables and plants in no time.

167
Gift Plants
http://www.nybg.org/plants/bestgift.html
Check out this list of the best houseplants to give during the year.

168
Garden and Flower Screen Savers and E-cards
http://www.123greetings.com/flowers
http://www.thegardenhelper.com/screensavers.html
http://www.spectrumsoftware3d.com/flowers.html
http://www.etera.com/club/screensaver.asp
Put the beauty of your garden on your computer screen, or share your love of flowers by sending a blooming e-card.

169
<u>Outdoor Flags</u>

http://www.ajflags.com
http://www.flags.com
http://www.festiveflags.com
http://www.islanderflags.com
http://www.mailorderflags.com/decorativecatalog.htm
Search these sites to find decorative flags to fly all year long.

170
<u>Garden Accessories</u>

http://www.smith-hawken.com
http://www.yardmart.com
http://www.winterthurgifts.com
http://www.jacksonandperkins.com
http://www.gardenleaf.com
Shop for mailboxes, birdbaths, fountains, address markers, garden plaques and many other outdoor accessories at these sites.

171
Pools and Spas

http://www.tutty.com/pools.htm
Dive into this virtual deep end and find out how to choose the right swimming pool or spa for your family. There is plenty of information on maintenance and upkeep, with links to manufacturers' and chemical makers' Web sites.

172
Gas Grills

http://www.bar-b-que.com
http://www.barbecuen.com
From a portable propane to a built in smoke pit, you can find barbecue solutions here.

CHAPTER VIII
HARDWARE, TOOLS AND MATERIALS

173
Tool Dictionary

http://www.sierra.com/sierrahome/homedesign/tool
Learn all about tools and their different uses.

174
Buying Guide

http://www.homewarehouse.com
You'll find a wide variety of tools, with reviews and a recommended buying guide here.

175
Tool Manufacturers

http://www.blackanddecker.com
http://www.dewalt.com
http://www.ridgid.com
http://www.sears.com/craftsman
http://www.ryobi.com
http://www.stanleyworks.com
http://www.klein-tools.com
Search interactive catalogs at these sites to find the tool that meets your particular need.

176
Shop for Hardware Online

http://www.acehardware.com
http://www.truevalue.com
http://www.amazon.com
http://www.sears.com
http://www.hardware.com
http://www.cornerhardware.com
Purchase hammers, nails and other hardware items at these informative sites.

177
Building Supply Connections

http://www.build.com
http://www.abuildnet.com
These are your Internet resources for millwork, molding and other building supplies. Enter what you need, and you'll be connected to suppliers in an instant.

178
Masonry and Concrete Basics

http://www.bhglive.com/homeimp/carpentry.html
Learn basic principles for laying brick, mortar and concrete.

HARDWARE
KITCHEN and BATH
LAWN and GARDEN

"With the right tools, I can fix anything...except my budget!"

179
Roofing

http://nrca.net/consumer
http://www.asphaltroofing.org
http://www.cedarbureau.org
http://gamma.rwu.edu/users/pcm/pub/slate/contents.html
Find the best roof for your house at these sites.

180
Insulation

http://www.ornl.gov/roofs+walls/insulation
Familiarize yourself with different types of insulation and how to soundproof your home.

181
Drywall

http://www.gp.com/build/gypsum/diy
http://www.national-gypsum.com
http://www.usg.com/remodcon.htm
Calculate how much wallboard you need for your next project, and learn how to install and repair drywall here.

182
Lumber

http://www.wwpa.org/techguide
Learn about the different grades of lumber and how to select the best wood products.

183
Brick and Siding

http://www.bia.org
http://www.vinylsiding.org
http://www.vinyl-siding.com
http://www.amazingsiding.com
Explore the benefits of brick and siding for your next home.

184
Synthetic Stucco

http://www.eifsfacts.com
Find out what the new and improved stucco can do for you. If you've had moisture problems
in the past, you can find solutions here.

185
Fireplace Mantels

http://www.mantels.net
http://www.mantelshop.com
http://www.oldworldstoneworks.com
Add distinction to a room with one of the unique mantels from these sites.

CHAPTER IX
NEW, REMODELED AND RESTORED

186
New Home Guide

http://www.nahb.com/consumers
The National Home Builder's Association provides objective advice for consumers about buying, building and renovating a home.

187
View House Plans Online

http://www.store.homestyles.com
http://www.dreamplans.com
http://www.dreamhomesource.com
http://www.designsplus.com
http://www.house-plan.net
http://www.coolhouseplans.com
http://www.hbrnet.com/homeplan
Do you wish you had a mud room, more storage or a larger kitchen? Review custom home plans and popular blueprints at these sites, and design the home of your dreams.

188
Log Home Plans

http://www.loghome.net
http://www.theloghomesite.com
http://www.cedarhomes.com
http://www.honka.com
http://www.xroads.net/cabinfever

Do you ever think about leaving the city or the suburbs for a quiet cabin in the woods? After you visit these sites, you'll see why cabins aren't just for country folk anymore.

189
Affordable Housing

http://www.nahn.com

If you think you can't afford a home, think again. It might not pay to rent with these energy efficient, low cost house plans available from the National Affordable Housing Network.

190
Custom Building

http://www.b4ubuild.com

Understand the custom building process by reading in-depth discussions of each stage from pre-construction to closing. View a sample construction schedule to find out how long it might take to build your new home.

191
Hiring an Architect

http://www.aiaaccess.com
This American Institute of Architecture site has twenty questions you should ask an architect, and tips for managing the building process.

192
Construction Answers

http://www.askbuild.com
This popular newspaper columnist can answer your building questions. Read his tips or search the archives for past articles of interest to you.

193
Find a Local Builder

http://www.homebuilder.com
http://www.builderdirectory.com
If you are looking for a builder, these sites offer a list organized by state. You can even view desirable communities online.

194
Better Business Bureau

http://www.bbb.org
Before you hire a contractor or builder, investigate his reputation with your local chapter of the Better Business Bureau.

195
National Association of the Remodeling Industry

http://www.nari.org
Search for award-winning designs and find new ideas for your home at this professional remodeling organization's site.

196
Manage Your Renovation

http://www.contractors.com/h_consumertips/consumertips.html
http://www.geocities.com/CapitolHill/6040/in01.htm
Manage you renovation process from beginning to end, and be prepared when inevitable problems arise with the help of these friendly, step-by-step guides.

197
Selecting A Contractor
http://www.411homerepair.com/contractor/tips.htm
http://www.contractors.com
Learn how to find a local contractor that's right for your project.

198
Contractor Agreement
http://www.ahahome.com/net_hi/index.html
Protect yourself by printing out an agreement before you contract your next improvement.
Also, enjoy interesting remodeling articles from the American Home Owner's Association.

199
Renovation and Building
http://www.dreamremodeling.com
Prepare yourself for the renovation and building experience. Learn how to identify land that
suits your construction plans and how to design a home to fit your family's needs.

200
Carpentry 101
http://www.bhglive.com/homeimp/carpentry.html
Whether you do it or not, this online tutorial will help you understand basic carpentry.

201
Remodeling Product Guides
http://remodeling.hw.net/guide
http://www.homesoft.com
Get the goods on remodeling products. Read reviews written about specific items and find out about new, cutting-edge products.

202
Remodeling Price Guide — Cost vs. Return
http://remodeling.hw.net/consumer/proto/costval/costval.htm
Before you remodel, determine how much to spend by taking a realistic look at what you are likely get to out of it. This guide analyzes the return on twelve projects in 60 cities across the U.S.

203
Avoid Home Repair Fraud
http://www.ag.state.il.us/facts/f-home.htm
http://www.fraud86.com
http://www.usps.gov/websites/depart/inspect/homeimpr.htm
Don't fall victim to home improvement fraud. Learn how to avoid scams that target homeowners. If you feel you've already been a victim of fraud, register a complaint.

204
Design a Deck

http://www.decksusa.com
View deck plans in 3D. If you like what you see, you can order the plans or software that can help make your custom deck a reality.

205
Build a Deck

http://www.bhglive.com/homeimp/decks.html
Here are complete instructions for building and designing most types of decks.

206
Remodeling

http://www.remodeling.com
Find budget information, design ideas, professionals, products and repair and maintenance advice at this comprehensive remodeling Web site.

207
Historic Restoration

http://www.traditional-building.com
http://www.rtis.com/reg/roundtop/kindlin1.htm
http://www.oldhouseweb.com
http://www.oldhousejournal.com
http://www.oldhousechronicle.com
http://www.rtsc.com
http://www.designsintile.com

If you're interested in restoring a historic landmark or fixing up an older home, these are indispensable resources.

CHAPTER X
MAINTENANCE, SAFETY AND REPAIR

208
Home Maintenance Tips

http://www.allabouthome.com/tips
http://www.mrclean.com
Find tips on cleaning, home safety, maintenance and prevention at this very consumer friendly site.

209
Fix it Yourself

http://www.doityourself.com
http://www.diyonline.com
Avoid a do-it-yourself debacle by reading the informative articles at these sites. You can solve your maintenance and repair dilemmas in a few clicks.

210
Learn How

http://www.learn2.com
These folks have tutorials for many home improvement projects.

211
Maintenance Answers

http://www.askme.com
http://www.ask.com
The best way to learn is to ask questions. These sites are ready, willing and able to assist.

212
Call the Home Doctor

http://www.homedoctor.net
Is your home healthy? Keep your residence allergy free and your appliances humming along.

213
Product Reviews

http://goodhousekeeping.women.com/gh/buysmart/guides/00buye21.htm
The Good Housekeeping Institute evaluates and reports on products for your home.

214
Toiletology 101

http://www.toiletology.com/index.shtml
Many of those perplexing little toilet problems can be solved with a few adjustments that don't require the help of a plumber. Learn basic toilet trouble-shooting at this must bookmark site.

"I can't start remodeling your kitchen
until you show me a permit...from your wife!"

215
Home Maintenance Encyclopedia
http://www.msue.msu.edu/msue/imp/mod02/master02.html
A large collection of objective home improvement and repair articles can be found at this
university Web site. Topics are alphabetically organized for easy reference.

216
Home Repair 101
http://homearts.com/helpers/homecare/hrec1.htm
Be prepared for the inevitable breakdowns in your house. Especially helpful is advice about
what to do in case of an emergency, such as when water pipes burst or a gas line leaks.

217
Pest Control
http://www.pestworld.org/homeowners
http://www.bugspray.com/articles/main.html
http://www.orkin.com
Learn how to eliminate pesky critters before they take over your house and yard.

218
Keep it Clean

http://www.4cleaning.com
http://www.organizedhome.com/clean/proclean.html
Keep your home cleaner, in less time, with the suggestions and useful product reviews at these sites. Also, find out if antibacterial soaps are really good for you.

219
Stain Removal

http://www.clothesline.com/stainDet
http://ext.msstate.edu/pubs/pub1400.htm
Don't get stressed by splatters and spills. Pick a stain and type of fabric, and these guides will help you get that stain out.

220
Cleaning Windows, Blinds and Curtains

http://housebeautiful.women.com/hb/decorate/maintain/00main44.htm
Cleaning blinds is necessary, but not necessarily fun. This site reveals the time-saving tricks of trained professionals so you can do it easier and faster.

221
Get Organized

http://www.organizedhome.com
http://www.123sortit.com
Gain control of the clutter in your home at these well-organized sites.

222
Storage Products

http://www.rubbermaid.com
http://www.getorginc.com
http://www.holdeverything.com
"I just don't have a place for everything!" Sound familiar? Find storage products to help you organize every room in your home.

223
Closets

http://www.closetmaid.com
http://www.customclosets.com
Discover space-saving tips, and design your closets online at these sites. You'll never dread opening that closet door again.

224
Safety Tips
http://www.lowes.com/lowes/findex.asp
Great home safety ideas are at this site, with seasonal advice and a must-do, top-twenty safety checklist for your home.

225
Baby Proof Your Home
http://www.babyproof.com
Young children are curious, and are therefore exposed to many hazards in the home you can't always anticipate. Make your home child-safe by following these room-by-room instructions.

226
Carbon Monoxide
http://www.freenet.msp.mn.us/people/guestb/pubed/cofaq.html
Get the facts on carbon monoxide. Find out why you should have a detector in your home, and where it should be mounted to protect your family.

227
Lead Paint
http://www.paint.org/con_info/pcle.htm
Could there be lead in your paint or in painted surfaces nearby? Learn how to avoid this toxic element and prevent lead poisoning.

228
Fire Safety
http://www.usfa.fema.gov/safety/safety.htm
http://www.ou.edu/oupd/fslist.htm
If you don't already have a fire escape plan, it's time to devise one. Learn how to plan the best escape routes, and where to store fire extinguishers in your home.

229
Energy Advisor
http://hes.lbl.gov
Enter your zip code to uncover the best ways to save energy in your specific climate. Also, compare your home energy bill to the average bill in your area.

230
Insulation
http://www.owenscorning.com/owens/around/insulation
Stay warm in the winter and cool in the summer. Find out about insulating your home.

231
Home Security
http://www.ncpc.org/1sec1dc.htm
http://www.ou.edu/oupd/hardhome.htm
Are you safe? Investigate the best ways to secure your property, and follow the detailed security checklists found at these sites.

232
Seasonal Maintenance Checklist
http://www.allabouthome.com/tips/seasonal/fall.html
http://www.newhome.on.ca/homeowners/main_manor/checklist_intro.htm
These convenient checklists show you what you should do each time the seasons change.

233
Weatherizing Your Home
http://www.doityourself.com/energy
http://www.homearts.com/pm/sweatequ/11weatf1.htm
http://www.learn2.com/05/0562/0562.php3
http://www.bbb.org/library/winterizing1099.asp
These handy guides can help you protect your home during inclement weather. Locate nooks and crannies and install quality weather stripping in an efficient, cost-effective way.

234
Prevent Water Damage
http://www.allstate.com/safety/home/safety.html
Follow the advice at this site to prevent water damage to your home. There are also instructions for what to do if your home suffers water damage.

235
All About Caulk
http://www.dap.com
http://www.ge.com/silicones/diy/homeprojectlibrary
Professional advice and products at these sites will help you seal up cracks and seams.

236
Improving Indoor Air Quality
http://www.epa.gov/iaq/is-imprv.html
How often should you get your air ducts cleaned? Find the answer and many other ideas to improve indoor air quality.

237
Heating and Cooling Advice
http://www.comfortnet.com/Homeowner_Index.htm
When your fan stops blowing, it may be a fuse, or you may need to call a repairman. Learn to recognize the difference at this site.

238
Replace a Faucet
http://www.nrha.org/howto/faucet/indxfct.htm
No more listening to "drip, drip, drip." Get instructions on how to fix and replace faucets.

239
Appliance Clinic
http://www.phoenix.net/~draplinc
For you diehard do-it-yourselfers, here's a guide to diagnosing and fixing your own household appliances. Rule Number One: Always Unplug!

240
Contact the Manufacturer
http://www.hangyourhat.com
No more waiting on hold; contact manufacturers online. The "Brand Rover" at this site provides links to most home product manufacturers' Web sites.

241
Recalls
http://www.cpsc.gov
Search for product recalls and report defective products at this U.S. Consumer Protection and Safety Commission site.

242
Garage Door Safety

http://www.amarr.com/safety/safety.html

Take a few minutes to test and properly maintain your garage door. Learn how at this site.

CHAPTER XI
FURNITURE

243
Furniture Buying Guide
http://www.homefurnish.com/buy_menu.htm
http://www.ianr.unl.edu/pubs/homefurnish/g1247.htm
When buying furniture, learn what to look for to select the best quality.

244
Arranging Furniture
http://www.sheffield.edu/link1/htmlsrc/link1.html
Learn the principles of furniture layout, like finding the right balance lines and planning for your family's traffic patterns.

245
Virtual Furniture Arranging
http://lhj.com/yourhome/furniture/index.htm
No need for unnecessary lifting. Make the most out of your personal space by arranging your furniture on the computer screen, until you find the layout that works best for you.

246
Shopping For Furniture

http://www.behome.com
http://www.living.com
http://www.furniture.com
http://www.goodhome.com
http://www.furnitureonline.com
http://www.furniturepoint.com
http://www.furniturefind.com
http://www.frontera.com
http://www.crateandbarrell.com
Browse for or buy furniture from these online retailers.

247
North Carolina Connection

http://www.ncfurnitureonline.com
http://ncnet.com/ncnw/furn-onl.html
Shopping for furniture bargains has never been easier. These sites provide links to deals on fine furniture from leading North Carolina furniture manufacturers and discount retailers.

248
Traditional Furniture

http://www.lanefurniture.com
http://www.lexington.com
http://www.thomasville.com
http://www.bakerfurniture.com
http://www.bassettfurniture.com
http://www.centuryfurniture.com
http://www.bernhardtfurniture.com
http://www.harden.com
http://www.lazyboy.com
http://www.drexelheritage.com
http://www.ethanallen.com
http://www.henredon.com
http://www.pennsylvaniahouse.com

You don't have to leave the house to window shop for furniture anymore. Search these online furniture makers' catalogs to find classic furniture for your home.

249
Furniture Care

http://www.fabriclink.com
http://www.homefurnish.com/woodcare.htm
http://www.furniture.com/magazine/leather101.asp
Keep your furniture in tip-top condition with the helpful advice from these sites.

250
Contemporary Furniture

http://www.pacecollection.com
http://www.storehousefurniture.com
http://www.dcuinc.com
http://www.bluedeco.com
These sites can help you fill your home with modern furniture.

"People are always tripping over
that step, so I installed an air bag."

251
Children's Furniture

http://www.kinderkraft.com
http://www.stanleyfurniture.com
http://www.kidsconvertibles.com
http://www.roomplus.com
http://www.bunksnstuff.com
http://www.bhome.com/bunkbeds.htm
http://www.bergfurniture.com
View and order furniture specifically for children and teens.

252
Need a New Mattress?

http://www.sealy.com
http://www.simmonsco.com
http://www.serta.com
http://www.kingsdown.com
These sites can help you sleep better. Compare brands from the comfort of your home.

253
Shop for Bedding and Accessories

http://www.thecompanystore.com
http://www.jcpenney.com
http://www.domestications.com
http://www.ultimate-outlet.com
http://www.target.com
http://www.landsend.com
http://www.llbean.com

Snuggle into new sheet and bedding ensembles available from these online retailers.

254
Rustic Furniture

http://www.lodgecraft.com
http://www.mountainelegance.com
http://www.lodgecreations.com

Search for rustic and log furniture at these sites.

255
Unfinished Furniture

http://www.unfinishedfurniture.org

Discover the benefits of real wood furniture, learn finishing tips and use the search feature to find an online dealer or locate a "brick and mortar" retailer near you.

256
<u>Office Furniture</u>

http://www.knoll.com
http://www.hermanmiller.com
http://www.techline-furn.com
http://www.ofconcepts.com
http://www.cf-direct.com
http://www.staples.com
http://www.officedepot.com
Whether you are setting up a home office or just need a new filing cabinet, you'll find many of your office needs here.

257
<u>Outdoor Furniture</u>

http://www.creativeplay.com
http://www.adirondackfurniture.com
http://www.cedarstore.com
http://www.thegardenroom.com
http://www.smith-hawken.com
http://www.backyardstore.com
Shop for new patio furniture today.

258
Antique Shopping Online

http://www.cyberattic.com
http://www.tias.com
http://www.antiqueozarks.com
http://www.antiqueweb.co.uk/welcomein.htm
http://www.antiques-avenue.com
http://www.antiquesonline.com.au
http://www.belgiumantiques.com
http://www.antiques-warehouse.com

From Maine to the Motherland, then Down Under and back to the Bayou, these sites hold the key to finding antiques all over the world.

259
Antiques Roadshow

http://www.pbs.org/wgbh/pages/roadshow/index.html

Maybe those pictures in the basement are worth something. Learn to look for treasure when cleaning out the attic, and read actual stories of great antique finds.

260
Antique Mall Directory

http://www.antiquemallsusa.com
Use this searchable index to locate antique stores and malls in your area, or in places you plan to visit. Just click on a state and a city, and you'll be directed to nearby antique stores in no time.

261
Antique Restoration

http://www.antiqueresources.com
Here's a comprehensive antique site with detailed information on antique restoration. You can even e-mail your difficult questions to the "Antique Doctor."

CHAPTER XII
RELOCATION AND REAL ESTATE

262
Real Estate Emporium

http://www.realtor.com

This is the Grande Dame of real estate sites on the Web. Search over one million home listings from around the country, including some you can virtually tour. Locate a realtor, lender and find an abundance of advice on buying or selling a home.

263
Relocation Information

http://www.homefair.com

If you are contemplating a move, start your research here. Compare communities, schools and salaries around the country.

264
Real Estate Advisor

http://homeadvisor.msn.com
http://realestate.yahoo.com

Explore neighborhoods, learn to negotiate the best price for a home, find a loan or view property listings here.

265
Open House Online
http://www.realestate.com
View real estate from coast to coast. This Web site walks you through the buying and selling process and espouses your financing options. You can also do an analysis to appraise your current property, or find out what it may be worth in a few years.

266
Find a Home
http://www.homes.com
Search through nationwide listings for the perfect home.

267
First Time Home Buyers
http://www.homepath.com
Get essential information for first time home buyers, with discussions of the pros and cons of home ownership, tips on choosing the right home and step-by-step explanations of the complete buying and loan closing process.

268
For Sale by Owner

http://www.owners.com

If you decide you're ready to sell your home yourself, this site has the info you need to close the deal. View national "For Sale By Owner" listings here.

269
Mortgages101

http://www1.lendingtree.com/new/resourcecenter/mortgage1.asp

http://www.mortgage101.com

http://www.hsh.com

Learn to lock in an interest rate, and how extra payments can pay off your mortgage early.

270
Find a Loan

http://www.countrywide.com

http://www.lendingtree.com

http://www.eloan.com

http://www.quickenmortgage.com

http://www.hfamerica.com

http://www.homefair.com/homefair/mortgage.html

http://www.mortgage-net.com

Pick a loan—refinance, mortgage home equity. Search many lenders for the best rate and use calculators to estimate how much you can borrow and what your payments will be.

271
Mortgage Rates

http://www.bankrate.com
http://www.americanloansearch.com
http://www.homeowners.com
Compare state mortgage rates and watch the market trends to secure the best financing.

272
Mortgage Calculators

http://www.realestate.com/calculators/home.asp
http://www.realtor.com/ResourceCenter/FinanceCenter.asp
http://homeadvisor.msn.com/ie/financing/calculators.asp
Calculators, a monthly expenditure worksheet, payment comparisons for different types of loans, and a breakdown of closing and other costs, can be found at these sites.

273
Avoid Common Mortgage Mistakes

http://www.mortgage-net.com/reference/top10.shtml
Read the top ten mistakes that people make when shopping for a new home, financing and refinancing. It'll save you money.

274
Name Your Own Mortgage Rate

http://www.priceline.com

Let the lenders come to you. State your rate and terms, then see if your offer is accepted. You'll know within six hours.

275
School Reports

http://www.theschoolreport.com

http://realestate.yahoo.com/realestate/schools

Evaluate the performance of public schools in your area, or the area that you are moving to.

276
Credit Report

http://www.experian.com/product/consumer

http://www.equifax.com

http://www.transunion.com/Consumer

http://www.ftc.gov/bcp/conline/pubs/credit/crdtdis.htm

At these sites, request a copy of your credit report and learn how to report credit errors.

277
Map Quest

http://www.mapquest.com
http://www.zip2.com
Get directions to a property, and check out its surrounding area.

278
Compare Cities

http://www.bestplaces.net
Find the best places for you to live, based on your lifestyle.

279
Insurance Quotes

http://www.quotesmith.com
http://www.insweb.com
http://www.insuremarket.com
http://www.insure.com/home/index.html
Get quotes for all of your insurance needs. You may be surprised.

280
Choose a Moving Company

http://www.moving.com
http://www.moverquotes.com
Evaluate moving companies, and get free estimates.

281
Moving Checklist

http://www.usps.gov/moversnet
Get free advice on such moving details as: changing your voter registration card, forwarding your mail, planning your travel route, helping prepare your kids and locating your new post office. There are even links to states' Motor Vehicle Licensing and Registration Web sites.

282
Inspect before You Buy

http://www.inspectamerica.com
http://www.builtonline.com/articles.cfm?P_ID=372
http://www.markw.com/10point.htm
http://www.homeinspect.org
Doing a proper home inspection can help you make a sound decision. These sites will help you evaluate your new dream home.

283
Guide to Buying a New Home
http://www.nahb.com/consumers/new_home/default.htm
Questions to ask a realtor, mortgage lender and property seller are listed here.

284
Home Selling Tips
http://www.homegain.com
http://www.realestate.com/selling/home.asp
Learn how to sell your existing home faster, with the advice and suggestions at these sites.

285
Consumer Information Center
http://www.gsa.gov/staff/pa/cic/housing.htm
Free consumer publications tell you how to buy a new home with information on adjustable rate mortgages, refinancing, mortgage lock-ins and how to negotiate a great deal.

286
Virtual Tours
http://www.bamboo.com
http://www.ipix.com
Virtually tour properties in over 5,000 cities around the world, using this state-of-the art Internet technology that can give you a 360-degree view of a home's interior and exterior.

"We'd like to find wallpaper to match the colors
in our carpet: brown dog hair, gray cat hair, yellow
mustard, red ketchup, blue clay, green finger paint...."

287
Real Estate Law

http://www.nolo.com/category/re_home.html

http://www.thelaw.com

If you have a legal question about real estate, these sites will probably have the answer.

288
Home Equity Loans

http://www1.lendingtree.com/new/resourcecenter/homeequity1.asp

If you're contemplating a home equity loan, this is the site for you.

289
Should I Refinance?

http://www.homepath.com/hrp1.html

http://quickenloans.quicken.com/Centers/refi.asp

Find out if refinancing will save you money. Consider some of the issues: out-of-pocket costs, interest savings and how long you plan to stay in your home.

290
Tax Information

http://www.relibrary.com/23main1.htm
Here's information that will help you understand your real estate taxes, with links to state and federal forms that you can print.

291
Foreclosures

http://www.foreclosureinfo.net
http://www.foreclosureworld.net
http://www.foreclosurecentral.com
Try your luck at finding a foreclosure bargain.

292
International Real Estate

http://www.escapeartist.com
http://www.ired.com
A villa in Tuscany? If you've ever dreamed of owning property abroad, you'll enjoy these sites.

293
Renting

http://www.apartmentguide.com
http://www.springstreet.com
http://www.rentconnection.com
Find an apartment or house to rent.

CHAPTER XIII
HOME HOBBIES AND CRAFTS

294
Habitat for Humanity

http://www.habitat.org
If you're handy around the house, try helping in your local community. Bring the family along.

295
Cooking

http://www.epicurious.com
http://www.foodtv.com
Tantalize your taste buds; try a new recipe.

296
Arts and Crafts

http://www.michaels.com
http://www.joann.com
http://www.crafterscommunity.com
Plenty of crafts, links and discussions for adults and children can be found at these sites.

297
Sewing

http://www.sewing.org
http://www.sewnews.com
http://www.sharewareplace.com/101/101sew.shtml
Find home sewing projects, how to measure for window treatments, bed covers, table toppers, and a fabric yardage conversion chart.

298
Photography

http://amateurphoto.about.com
http://www.eframe.net
These sites can help you take better pictures and find funky frames.

299
Woodworking

http://www.woodnet.net
http://www.taunton.com/fw
http://www.kiva.net/~rjbrown/w5/wood.html
Here are projects, plans and tips for all of your woodworking needs.

300
Collecting

http://www.icollector.com
http://www.collectoronline.com
http://www.collectit.net
http://www.the-forum.com
Look for rare and valuable collectibles at these sites.

Index (by site number)

INDEX (BY SITE NUMBER)

Index (by Site Number)

The Incredible Newsletter

If you are enjoying this book, you can also arrange to receive a steady stream of more "incredible Internet things," delivered directly to your e-mail address.

The Leebow Letter, Ken Leebow's weekly e-mail newsletter, provides new sites, updates on existing ones and information about other happenings on the Internet.

For more details about *The Leebow Letter* and how to subscribe, visit us at:

WWW.300INCREDIBLE.COM